Bio

INVENTORY PRESS

Bio

MARYAM MONALISA GHARAVI

Possessor of a

tel
ence
phalon

and

highly opposable

thumbs

Only daughter of an

only daughter of an

only daughter

The battle to compose life
is daily fought between
rhopography and
megalography,

between the merits of the
trivial and mundane
against the heroic and
important

No forced ha

ha's,

only authentic ha

ha's

What if the difference between biography and autobiography were like the one between jail and prison?

In one summary detention.

The other, prolonged conviction.

Containing

live
fires

MAY 6

News?

I had no expectation
of news

Maybe it unsettles you
now

but

        every real beginning
requires a real ending

Wild and varied dreaming.

Refresh,
delete,
delete,
delete,
close tab,
scroll down,
expand,
select,
highlight,
copy,
scroll up,
new tab

MAY 10

A donkey will mother almost any animal

Should I be trying to "own"
it?

What are the terms
of ownership?

What is
"it?"

Erring

and/
or

caring

MAY 13

Films, like ______________,

have to be finished

How
about

we

didn't

It's not you,
it's not me,

it's capital

and cops

Face veils are really in right now

This month I operated
power tools for the first
time.

It may sound delusional
but I experienced them as
tools that make you feel
powerful

Rushing less and less

to fill irreducible voids

I am fine
to drink my wine.

I have glee
to drink my tea.

I've the wits
to drink my spritz.

MAY 20

We can self-complete

when we're

dead

MAY 21

I
make

my
self

see
ing

MAY 22

Passport renewal services,

un in cor po rated
terr it orie s

Femmephilia

in a femmephobic

world

MAY 24

"And there was always somebody calling you on the telephone, to interrupt the fantasies of suicide"

(Audre Lorde on the working definition of a friend)

Ca
ra
ca
,

mané

...

A suggestion
box

like at Qalandiya
                Checkpoint,

        only

a bio
        graphy

Communication   never
ceases

                to

                                        mis-

                        MAY 28

A soft spot

for

quitting

stories

MAY 29

How to Wear a Mask

(physician's office poster /
alternative book title)

MAY 30

Mud
mud der
mur   der; and other

Hitchcockian themes

Never   not leaving;

al ways

                    al ready

on

                    ar rival

Tehran Savings
& Loans, LLC

JUNE 2

New

kids on the

black

b
l
o
c

Saudade is Portuguese for

the wrangling haul of
cardboard boxes

and the

brevity of feeling

settled

Head

less

poet

Butter knives and machetes,

in a particular order

JUNE 6

Anti- social

media or

non-

mediated sociality

are

further options

I placed a self
on the internet

and watched it spread

This is impacting my schedule

Desirous of

    making only
things of no value, or
  more extremely,

        non-value
  itself

Better a blind sailor
near shore

or
a seeing swimmer
lost

at sea?

A teen hotline for people in their late twenties and early thirties

JUNE 12

Clean windows are
dangerous:

                    just ask the
young bird who learns the
mechanics of flight in the
safety of classroom
instruction

Treason

in the age of military dominance

JUNE 14

Capture,

log,
assemble,

con

ceal,

export

Going to tell it on the
mountain

so it can go tell it on the
molehill

You say "cry
like a baby"
like any adult actually
ever did

Run,

Mona,

run

Courting betrayal

JUNE 19

Always procedure,
always process.

Sometimes proscenium,
sometimes project.

Ex
tempore

JUNE 21

In/ process

and/ or

out/ bound

JUNE 22

Clocks reset, so

hopeful

become

ever

lasting

JUNE 23

A 1-800 number

reaching
back and
forward into
previous and
                                future

centuries

A dictionary in reverse, defining public terms in a private language

Images disguised

as speech

acts

JUNE 26

Seduction by falsetto

Every
day

the encounters

with the falsity

all around

us

Changing color   in a dark,
                          oceanic

                          cave,

like a private

                    amphibian

If office-bound, not

offing

but

offlining

Don't age, don't age, God

forbid

you

age

An exegesis
on the femininity
of men

I asked him about the we
in his I
and he said

yes,
I come from that

JULY 3

A supercut of
every time you've spelled
out

your full name

Where do all the unregistered acts of violence go?

Must only the morgue and the mother keep a record?

Stone

thrower

JULY 6

Killing all   my illusions

        used to matter

most;

        sometimes, now,

                just

better illusions

The enemy
of my enemy
is my face

Is "form"
another word
for fashion
?

Should you make
the terrible mistake of
having heroes,
ensure

that you never meet them

What

center?

Whose

center?

Why

center?

"Sometimes certain words
remain, like towers."

(Henri Michaux)

Airless

screams

into a screen

JULY 13

Certainty spells the
death
of an
artist

To find
in the movement and
cacophony of the crowd a
certain stillness

Arrangement of

rhythms

in an embodied

order

On every
page there
was a name,   black
ink set off by
the silence of   white

matter

Thanatos
in the 21st
century

is the equivalent of
the bombing
of tombs

JULY 19

JULY 19

Words begin to   lose

their earning,

        each syllable

detaching from

        its account

Even the most false,
clumsy
equivalence can be

instructive

Like a film residue, obsolescence

persists

JULY 22

An affect
in perpetual flux, a

zig

zagging county
road

The consequence of blank
ink on white paper,

the consequence of white
chalk on a blackboard

Can you
want

what you
get?

If you scratch hard
enough, as a reaction to
the magnitude of human
cruelty, maybe eventually
you find a way to crawl out

and exit your skin

No

one

cares

JULY 27

Even
her "whatever"s
were

loaded

You'll never be more

____

and

____

than you are
at this very moment

JULY 29

Un
commons

We are at
peak

bull

shit

JULY 31

Loss is a deletion with its
own accretive trace

Are we care yet

Year-round

fresh

produce

AUGUST 3

Don't be alarmed:

these crying spells and
    gasping sobs are just bi-

products of our current
    century

Re

dacting
    every
thing for the

              sake of safe

      keeping

Usually involves deletion
or substitution

of names   and other
key details

In the hex trade

AUGUST 7

No one rests

and much

less

in peace

Always putting society in quotation marks

If this is home,

we'd like to
be the first

to welcome
you

home

Wayward aliens that develop feelings on earth

AUGUST 11

She died
as she lived,

bludgeoned
by the empty

criminalization of
everything

Trying to keep warm in a
cold   and indifferent
world   full of
injustice and   bad
news

The whole business as

awful

after awful,

loss

after loss

Deep-earth goneness, like an abandoned   nuclear code

A highly publicized press
conference

slowly dismantling

the authorities, the police,
the stock market,
the press room furniture,

and finally
itself

The officer fired

several more
shots

The answer is

always yes, yes,   yes,
no,   no, no

Ensuring the unensured since 1492

No charges filed against the officer

AUGUST 20

Never not
nowhere,

trained in
the science of care

AUGUST 21

Between

my being

and the other's

being

The days move faster and
faster now,

the nights pacing
afoot at uneasy leisure

No rest
for the worse

for the wear

Survive attack

A series of crudely drawn
halos

over the heads of
outlaws

Ramallinha,
Ramallá

AUGUST 27

Escape

is a crescent
shape

Girls?

He dated six

at a time.

But he was scared of
women.

A radio,
a clock,
a phone,

all without batteries

Relocation,

relocation,

relocation

AUGUST 31

If true
it were

a lost paradise

SEPTEMBER 1

Captain Obvious, Major Duh, Sergeant No Really

The children were simply inconsolable

Taking the red pill
like Keanu

Are you aware
of the existence   of your
            own battalions

It constituted a privacy

of a very public sort

The difference between
an adapter
and   a converter

Guard your labor,
gird your grind,

spare the moil,
and spoil the mind

Time is never

our friend

Never one to resist
the smoldering vibrancy of
a syllabus

Unclad bather of either sex

SEPTEMBER 11

The wedding of
sweet water
and
salt water

The internet experience
as an unsettling
dream

whereby the contents
are forgotten

but the sensorial effects
linger

SEPTEMBER 13

A container of

p(r)o
(b
l)ems

Anchored,   anchored,

ancora

First as shadow play, then
as captured light, then

as algorithms of zeroes
and ones

Serum,
scripture,
wall;
a free

lunch,
some portraits,
a charity

deposit box

“Let us make ourselves
extinct”

(only lines printed on Khalil
Sakakini's carte de visite)

An otherness
without wildness

Subdued trauma on the
faces   all
around

                    me

Sea against
the mountain

The ride is nice
but I want it

to be faster

and wilder

They tired

of news,

where violence

was both   subject and

delivery mechanism

Somewhere beneath

layers of self-denial,
            negation, and
doubt

                    lay the point

The essay as geography-less travelogue

A banquet

without plates,

a visitation
without a host

"Nuclear"
families

eventually explode

The spectators frantically
escaped

                    the theater for
fear of getting wet

from the stormy sea
                    onscreen

Art must
n't must

Institute of Solo Acts in Many Parts

SEPTEMBER 30

An enemy project,
and other
costume possibilities

The return of those who never left

OCTOBER 2

A militarized suburban
corridor

on the edge of your gold
nation

In art and empire
there was the open
secret,

in only one a set of
electronic eyes

The ability to dole out
scrutiny and empathy with
genuine care for that
enterprise

A sniper

atop

a concrete citadel

watched the moving ants
below,

eating

a bag of stale chips

and flipping through
his phone

OCTOBER 6

Glamour and sweat, often

and early

Beginnings:
Morning coffee,
open window,
solar eclipse, and one

imaginary ocean
gleaming

What if you couldn't
assuage the cries

the chained

dog

or free him

Always a system
in place even

if arbitrary

The unalloyed d r e a   d
that covers   e v e r
y thing

And then we walked
our separate ways, like the
humanities and the
sciences

Belief and disbelief in
poetry amount to the same
thing.
		Thankfully,
since it doesn't need either

The name for a Rashomon device before the creation of Rashomon

"I might now introduce myself—to myself, first and foremost, it occurs to me"

(Iris Murdoch, *The Sea, The Sea*)

A little bit

every
day

or
all at once

But her comrade game was on point

In the heavy wave of the
midnight rush

I

forgot myself
and wrote myself

The authorities,
who sprayed the hostile
object,
            cautioned

                        against

alarm

Unexplainable acronyms

and other unmarked vehicles

Human economy from wholesale to   retail to freebie bin

Mere satrap of
the disappeared gods

A crowd is

a utopian

project

The difference between a
strategy and a tactic, in
that
        a tactic enters
                    the other's

space

High thread count
where   it counts

You and your shadow in lifelong selfless marriage

The wave crested   up,   up

in my coffee

                                    cup

I gather all   of myselves,
they try to   escape
con tain men t

Defining things by what
they are not,   e.g.
a door   is not a window

The fugitive appeared
from the dark to break
the silence

A snow-capped mountain landscape

printed on a 24% annual percentage rate credit card

The bizarre menace of someone repeating your name

in every sentence

Utilize! Expedite! Officiate!

Expand!

"Among the beamlike
spears of the enemies
stand close, securely"

(Archilochus)

The harder

the fight

the greater

the insight

They spoke calmly of
their death, as if

they knew it, as if
it had appeared to them

Everything on permanent
delay,   like a train
conductor confused by
          how long one should
pause   at the tracks

The air I'm breathing   isn't
really

mine

Two monsters conjoined: fear of the unknown and the desire for certainty

Guarding the greatest

gifts closely

so

they can be given away

freely

as desired

Every battle was worth the wars lost

An earthquake that
shatters

everything but birds' nests

My elegy   for your ode,
your epic   for my ballad

I gush

right through   your fiber-

        optic   net

work

                        cables

A telephone attracting
more   wrong
numbers and missed calls

            than actual
            conversations

A family resemblance

between thinking
and fog

To our parents,

to whom we owe
the curse and gift of
existence

International Union of
Items Crossed Out
from a List

NOVEMBER 17

A plausible, fully articulated hypothesis about how a phenomenon occurs

To give birth to our
selves
in the color
blue

An ellipsis
inside
a thought   bubble
placed over my head

Ten se   vers   a tile

Vast territory between "sell

out" and

"sold

out"

Thick and tight like
a stack of fresh
envelopes

A critic
named Jeremiad

In the room the colonial
settlers come and go

Talking of Michelangelo

Mittelschmerz but

for every heavily released
feeling

A city   mar
red and   unprotected, like
an   open face in the gust

Dial tone followed by
voicemail greeting on a
911 emergency line

Centenaries of restless
searching,

après Ogum and Ulysses

Prayer for safe voyage in
your honor,

a humble propempticon for
every possible treachery
on the way

The good strife

Hands in the act of
enfolding   other hands,

surrounded   in grey
shadow

DECEMBER 2

In wearing the gypsum
mask   I feared
becoming   one with it

Everything looks dirtier
the more you stay
at home

Too much poetry
was never the problem,
too much   cruelty was

I sit tightly
in my puddle,

surveying the field of
flying bullets

Do you even know who

I'm

not?

Who

do you think   you

aren't?

Notes on a mortal and irrational condition

DECEMBER 8

A young boy named

Mater
Protectrix

Mohammad so-and-so

A night run,
a low moon, a tinted
car window

Spirit l

strong distilled
volatile substance

DECEMBER 12

Not FREEDOM TO
or

FREEDOM FROM
but

FREEDOM FOR

Pyramid

scream

Toilet manufacturers Imperial, Inc.

To acquire a deep sleep
state in non-sleep

A well-developed trigger
finger, muscular
and taut

Grounded in

groundlessness

DECEMBER 18

Airlifted to

airlessness

The best offense

is good

suspense

A new moon in or

bit   before you

were ready to give up

                  the old one

Promissory by nature, precautionary by nurture

Somewhere,

a someday somehow somewhens

And
work
will
make
you
flee

All forms speak of
themselves and
their counter form

New! Grief
in 26 languages

For a limited time, letters to the editor will be considered for publication

at 50% off

There are mortals

on the ground and ghosts

in the trees and police
in the bushes

An earthquake
struck the city with crime,
lassitude,   and illness

Please excuse our face!

We're renovating

DECEMBER 30

In certain places,

time takes longer

to pass

Umm Harb

In Aeminium,
lusophonically speaking

Dreams as
the finely spun fairytale

gold of real life

Invent nothing but reinvent

e v e r y

thing

A dozen   eggs

in hard angle

to your sun

A to-do list for the apocalypse, and other burning ships

Any machine can perform
a task,   only a
human being can   work

They come
for blood, and when all the
blood is drained

they take the soil, and
when all the soil is
unearthed

they give it their name

The feedback

QR code

scanner

at airport

security

Circus world of cheapened life, some more discounted than others

Something
has to be done,

before
the catastrophe

The airport's lack of smell is a smell

ONE-DAY ONLY SALE!

Budget funeral for the revolution season

JANUARY 13

You wouldn't like that
place,

dear,

that's where

only men go

When they
         bring guns,
                  bring your s
calpel

Extreme example of a half-serene, half-torrential micro half-climate

Strangers here

are much more likely to

help

a foreigner

in distress

than   is the case

back

home

History as patented sorrow

Herc

Kool
taught
me

JANUARY 19

Who says   says who?
Nobody   who is

anybody

A sustained and
methodical argument,
foremost with the self,

not obliging
victory or defeat

A secret friendship
            between truth and
half-

            truth

Poetry is the boundary
without

a frontier

Tonight at 11:

the shocking story of our imperial ambitions

JANUARY 24

The egg hatched a red

finch that slipped through
our fingers

and flew away

A new and
improved

enhancement

An unspecific past hurtling
toward an

in

de ter mi na te   future

The cunning moss
overgrown above us,

we doused the ground fire
with gasoline

The last outlaw

wasn't

hard to find

Cool body

locked in

tight

for a mind

to stay   heated

open wide

It's either the end of something

or the middle of nothing

A culture of camouflage

FEBRUARY 1

A navigational device
for earth's   slow
descent   into Hades

The vacuum-sucking
sound   the centrifuge
of the soul

          makes when
managing social toxicity

Measuring all distances in kilometers from

Jerusalem

FEBRUARY 4

Photographs captioned by
date, time, specification,
size, and pain expenditure

A dance   rhythmically

undressing

                    the spectator

FEBRUARY 6

Merely the inside of an
unknowable skull

laden with storms

Conduct unbecoming

the process

of becoming

Trees are mortal,
plastic
is evergreen

They ate horses and
rode cows,

they drew with fish and
caught pencils

From earth they came and to earth they shall return, so I take nothing with me

Irreconcilable

de
pen
den
ces

FEBRUARY 12

A bayonet   dispensed

from the back of a hoofed
animal

Promotional material for the end-of-humanity

Apocalypse Sale

FEBRUARY 14

The space of social
interrogation,

the space of waiting,

the space of event

Dust on the high

seas

It's all moving very fast
now, irrevocably

fast,

                    and slowness

can't be reinvented

Not not-
here, just

there there

Syn
chronized

jailhouse

dance

FEBRUARY 19

Girl Power anthems for a feudal age

You can always go

to the sea again

I renovate,
I renew,
I remake

myself
every day

The news cycle as ambient horror

Not silence

per se

but a tunnel

that swallows all

speaking voices

A terraced landscape,
undifferentiated in its
continual continuity

except for telephone
towers pricking up from
gray heights

A mislabeled jar of fear,

proudly displaying
other emotional feats

Unspooling the zygote

Union of dread and   bliss
in between slurps of

breath

That studying crow,
hungry

                and bequeathing gifts
to the feeder

An announcement from
Death's preselection
committee

that I am a finalist,

but there will be delays in

declaring the day's
winning candidates

Is newness bestness?

Adding "neo-" to almost
any word

                    makes it pejorative

The forced intimacy of a beheading

MARCH 4

Presence may be
overlooked

but every absence has an
explanation

MARCH 5

Sometimes the suffering seems insurmountable

When candid

accumulation,

when covert

dispossession

Be careful
that in the act of warming
you don't singe

Stealth

is
the new health

A bewildered ear
desperately

trying to close
its outer chamber

A real cat meets a
cartoon cat, and
unrequited love is
born

(but love was
always mediated)

A molehill, a vortex,

maelstrom of
metaphoric possibility

The relentless pursuit of
shelf space,   the urgency
of guarded footing

The word "modern" as a mask to hide cruelties and high crimes

We are a _____ family

Time is

the only thing

that makes no

sense

at all

MARCH 16

Disown

but never disarm

You can really afford to get wild with it

In the opening scene, the flight attendant offers a refresh towel to a passenger,

whose blanket falls away to reveal shackled hands

Mercurial suppositions

MARCH 20

As though always
                  brave,
     already

          free

A biological desire-
generating

machine
equipped with more

imagination
than logic

He raises his hands at the
airport body scanner
as an arrest reflex

Now search, now sigh

Innocuous emergencies

MARCH 25

Precipitated by an
interruption

in my friendship
with the dictionary

A place of small and petty
bigness whose jagged hills
overwhelm the outsider

All endowed by certain and uncertain terms

U n s p oo ling sweet lies

Airplane baby,
drone adult,
helicopter elder

Everything   sprayed with
        rose   water,
especially my

                      face

Long-term goals wearing
short-term goal dresses,
getting cat-called by
immediate goals

Comments are closed, submissions are open

Tears as biology,

tears as drama,

tears as
political currency

A rumor whose hour of alarm has come

To wrap oneself tightly
in the shrouds of the new,

the impossible desire to be

cloaked in clean
newness every waking day

APRIL 5

We have been urgently
trying to reach you, and
now that you're here, we
appreciate your patience

Not animation   per se,
but   surely   an

   animated   situation

A wolf named Grief,

proficient in a language
        called Foundling

Exit strategy: loop

adinf i n i tum

Record of a   disappearing
public

accumulation

A tale told by a fury

APRIL 11

It can't
all be
reduced
to this,

can it?

APRIL 12

In our predicament of liquidity   lies

the controlled hysterics of opera

superlative,
mights

Anti-
human

APRIL 14

Duetwell

About you

          I have been knowing,

hereon

                    toward

Ministry of Interiority

APRIL 17

Extant notes
to a lulled
ending

Com press ion   omics

APRIL 19

Land &
sea &
care

APRIL 20

Congratulations

on

your

recent labor

Desire
meets

ungovernability

Unincorporated future productions

APRIL 23

Leaving
something   undone in the

gap   before the fill

To be or not

to be   missed!

The completeness of the animal

woven into

silence

Glottal stops
on a l o n   g lingual tour

APRIL 27

2 Spastic, 2 Spurious

APRIL 28

Everybody out here

knows

somebody

who

All this time I was here,
waiting for you
to shed the coat
of helplessness

Staying loose with hard goodbyes

MAY 1

Maryam Monalisa Gharavi is an artist, poet, and theorist. Her work in film, video, performance, text, photography, drawing, and sound explores the interplay between aesthetic and political valences in the public domain. She completed a PhD at Harvard University, an MFA at Milton Avery Graduate School of the Arts at Bard College, and a BA at University of California-Berkeley. Prior book publications include a translation of Waly Salomão's *Algaravias: Echo Chamber* (Ugly Duckling Presse), *The Distancing Effect* (BlazeVOX), *Apparent Horizon 2* (Bonington Gallery), and *Alphabet of an Unknown City* (Belladonna*).